JUNIOR SURVIVAL LIBRARY

The World's Wild Dogs

THE WOLF

Jeremy Bradshaw

Irwin Publishing
Toronto, Canada

Key to abbreviations

g	gram
kg	kilogram
cm	centimetre
m	metre
km	kilometre
km²	square kilometre
km/h	kilometres per hour

Copyright © 1992 by Irwin Publishing
First published in 1991 by Boxtree Limited,
London, England
Copyright © 1991 Survival Anglia Limited
Text copyright © 1991 Jeremy Bradshaw

Front jacket photograph:
Survival Anglia/Claude Steelman
(An Arctic wolf)
Back jacket photograph:
Survival Anglia/Richard and Julia Kemp
(A group of wolves in northern Spain)

Line drawings by Wayne Ford

Edited by Cheryl Brown
Designed by Glynn M. Pickerill
Typeset by Rowland Phototypesetting Limited
Bury St Edmunds, Suffolk

Printed and bound in Italy
by OFSA s.p.a.

for Irwin Publishing,
1800 Steeles Avenue West
Concord, Ontario
Canada
L4K 2P3

Canadian Cataloguing in Publication Data
Bradshaw, Jeremy
   The world's wild dogs : the wolf.

(Junior survival library)
Includes index.
   ISBN 0-7725-1892-0 (bound)   ISBN 0-7725-1893-9 (pbk.)

1. Wolves – Juvenile literature.   I. Title.
II. Title: The wolf.   III. Series: Junior
survival library (Toronto, Ont.).

QL737.C22B73 1992   j599.74'442   C91-094548-9

Contents

The world's wild dogs

The wild dogs of the world—the wolf, the coyote, the dingo and the jackal—roam some of the wildest parts of the earth. The wolf survives in much of the northern hemisphere, including the snowy wastes of the High Arctic, where it hunts musk ox and caribou; the yelling howl of the coyote can be heard across North America from Alaska to Mexico City; the dingo, introduced into Australia by early humans, runs wild across the dusty red outback; while the jackal is at home on the wide grassy plains of Africa among milling herds of antelopes and prides of lions.

Wild dogs have many features in common. They all have long tails, which are often bushy, and tapered triangular ears. They are friendly to other members of their family and take great care of their young. They have 42 teeth with sharp canines for gripping **prey** and broad molars for chewing food. Their claws are strong and blunt, and these always show in their tracks because they cannot be **retracted**. With their slender muscular bodies and long legs, wild dogs are some of the strongest runners in the animal kingdom.

Wolves in the evergreen oakwoods of northern Spain. The wolf is now extinct in most European countries.

A black-backed jackal near a waterhole in Etosha National Park, Namibia in southern Africa.

Wild dogs are members of the canid family, a group of dog-like creatures which includes the fox. Foxes differ from wild dogs in several ways, however: they tend to be smaller; they are not so sociable; and they seldom hunt in packs. Canids are **carnivores**. Although you may not have seen a wild dog, you are sure to have met one of their close relations, for the domestic dog was once a wolf. Early humans took wolves from the wild and bred them for their own purposes. Among other things they selected those wolves that barked rather than howled. But on occasion our pet dogs can still be heard howling—a reminder of their distant past. It has taken thousands of years to tame the domestic dog, to create the variety of breeds we have today, and to establish the temperament of the family pet— playful, affectionate and loyal. The wild dogs of the world remain fiercely wild: they will attack other dogs that are not part of their pack; and if they are hungry they will kill any animal that they think is worth eating.

As human populations have increased, they have settled most of the earth's wildernesses. From the beginnings of civilization wild dogs have been viewed by humans as competitors, because they live off prey animals such as deer which humans like to hunt too. As the wild dogs' natural prey diminished due to the effects of their human neighbours, they were driven to attack domestic stock, such as cattle and sheep. Because of this, humans have persecuted and sometimes completely exterminated the wild dogs from some areas. In fact they now occupy only a third of their original **range**. As the world's untouched areas continue to shrink, the future of wild dogs looks uncertain.

The howl of a wolf or the yell of a coyote is an eerie sound. It is the spirit of an animal that once ran free throughout the world's wildernesses. Humans have felt threatened by wild dogs in the past. But it is not too late for us to learn to co-exist with them, nor for us to realize that they symbolize the freedom of the wild places we are losing so fast.

Where wolves live

Wolves are animals of the north. They are found in three continents: North America, Europe and Asia. They circle the northern hemisphere from Alaska to Greenland and Siberia to Kamchatka. They live from the Arctic Circle, south to the deserts of Arabia. Wolves are truly versatile and adaptable animals. Throughout their range, they are probably most at home in forests. This is because there are large animals to hunt, and shelter. But in the southern part of their range in the US and Arabia, wolves scratch a living in semi-desert conditions. Wolves vary in size enormously, from the small steppe wolf, through the medium-sized European wolf, to the large tundra wolf which can reach a length of 2 m from nose to tail tip, and weigh up to 45 kg.

While wolves exist over a large area of the world, they have been eliminated from many parts of their range by humans. For centuries we have ruthlessly poisoned and trapped them because when wolves are hungry they kill domestic stock. In some places, like Japan, the wolf is already extinct. In North America wolf numbers have been decimated. Today, the best places to find America's grey wolf are in Canada (Alberta and British Columbia), and in Alaska and Minnesota in the US. There are some in Mexico, including the fringes of Mexico City itself. A second species of wolf, the smaller and rare red wolf, can be found in south-eastern US, but it is now almost exterminated in the wild.

Perhaps there is no better example of the wolf's persecution than the treatment it received in Europe. There were once wolves in every European country, but over the centuries they have been eliminated from most of them. A scattered few remain in the Abruzzi mountains of Italy. Scandinavia fights a battle to stop people killing its last survivors. Northern Spain has the best population, with

The Mexican wolf. There are probably fewer than one hundred of this subspecies left in the wild.

A lone wolf high in the Gredos mountains of central Spain.

perhaps 1500 individuals in the mountains of Cantabria and in Galicia. Of the several million wolves once in Europe, there are now probably less than ten thousand.

Folk stories of the 'big bad wolf' have given the animal a bad image. But the fact is that wolves avoid humans if they can. Old beliefs die hard, however, and there are still too many people who believe that the only good wolf is a dead wolf. It takes time to change attitudes. Thankfully steps are being taken to try to secure the wolf's future and it is now a protected species in much of Europe.

Werewolves

Werewolves are imaginary creatures. They are human beings that can at times turn into wolves, particularly under the light of a full moon. A werewolf is said to do the work of the devil—raiding graveyards and eating corpses. In medieval Europe people were tried by courts as werewolves and if found guilty were burned alive. The North American Indians' word for a wolf is the same as their word for witch. A Navajo Indian becomes a witch by putting on a wolf skin. In cases such as these the wolf has been used as a symbol to represent evil—a fate which it doesn't deserve.

At one time the wolf existed throughout the northern hemisphere, across all the shaded area on this map. It is now extinct over much of its former range, and today can only be found in the darker shaded area.

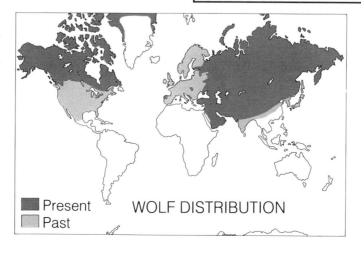

■ Present
▨ Past

WOLF DISTRIBUTION

The wily wolf

Wolves are elusive, secretive and shy animals. Even people who have spent their lives studying wolves have seen them hardly at all. At one time, the North American wolf expert David Mech had encountered only a dozen wolves in 20 years of research and study. In Spain a wildlife biologist who spent two years searching for wolves failed to catch sight of a single individual, although he knew from their tracks that they were there.

Without a doubt it is the wolf's highly-developed senses of hearing and smell that allow it to go unseen, thereby increasing its

Wolves usually hide in cover; their coats give them excellent camouflage.

success as a hunter. Wolves can hear the slightest sound—a deer breaking a twig for example—up to 3 km away. They can also hear sounds that humans cannot. For example, they can detect bats squeaking in **ultrasound**. It is said that a wolf's nose is long to give it a good sense of smell. In fact a wolf has a long muzzle to accommodate its powerful jaws and teeth with which it kills its prey. But their sense of smell *is* better than most. There is no doubt that wolves recognize hundreds of thousands of different smells which humans cannot. They move in a 'river' of scents which give them vital information in the tracking of their prey. By its acute sense of smell a wolf can tell which type of deer has been along a path, and when. Was it with a fawn? Where has it gone to? Is another wolf after it? A wolf is always in search of clues. Its superb hearing and smell more than compensate for its sight which is very poor. A wolf is much more likely to smell its prey than to see it.

Wolves' coats vary enormously in colour through their range. Arctic wolves are often white.

Wolf fur

Wolves can exist in the chilling cold of the Arctic, where the sun may not be seen for months in the winter, and in the driving rains of British Columbia. In these conditions soaking fur close to the skin would mean certain death in temperatures which can fall to −46°C. The wolves' two-layered fur keeps out the wet and the cold. Close to their skin they have soft, dense underfur. Then on the outside are long 'guard' hairs which have the remarkable ability to shed water before the underfur gets wet. In snow, rain or sleet the water is repelled by the guard hairs. A wolf can sleep out in the open on the tundras of Canada and Russia if need be, although it is more likely to find a snow hole or a cave in the rocks in which to shelter.

Arctic wolves are white so that the animals they hunt cannot see them. Wolf fur has been highly prized by people for hats and coats. Today public opinion is turning against the use of animal furs.

Another factor in the success of the wolf to go undetected is the colour of its coat. To the south of its range the wolf's coat is a sandy-grey colour blending in with the grass and rocks. To the north, the wolves' coats range from white on the tundra to black in the forests. In other words they are **camouflaged**.

The wolf is an extremely intelligent creature and it is the cleverest member of the canid family. In the Abruzzi in central Italy, the wolves know there are scraps to be had in the mountain villages but they wait until the villagers are safely in bed and until the last light has gone out before coming down to **scavenge** in the village. By dawn they are safely back in the hills. This adaptable behaviour has been crucial to the wolf's survival.

The wolf pack

Wolves are like human beings in several respects—they like to do things in groups but to be individuals too. The wolf pack contains between three and 25 individuals, with five or six as the average. Within the pack there are different personalities. Some are more aggressive, some are more placid. Some are bolder, some are more intelligent. Some are better at stalking prey, others at outrunning it. Like human teams, there are places for different skills within a group which has a common purpose. In the wolf's case the purpose of the pack is simple. The group is for hunting. Several wolves hunting together can bring down larger prey animals than a lone wolf hunting on its own.

The pack is led by a top male and a top female. These are not necessarily larger animals than the other members of the pack, but ones that have established their position through contests of strength and cunning (see box). They are always fully adult animals. Then there are other adults—often wolf cubs from the previous year which are now well grown. Finally there are the new cubs which may or may not be large enough to go hunting.

The size of the pack can vary considerably. In general wolf packs tend to be large in places where prey is large. Packs of 36 have been seen in Canada where they hunt North America's largest deer, the moose, which can weigh up to 800 kg. As a rule, however, wolf packs are getting smaller. This is partly

A dominant wolf snarls over another pack member it has forced into a submissive position.

Three male wolves smell a female's scent. A raised tail is often a sign of dominance.

because individuals are shot or poisoned, and partly because large prey is becoming more scarce. But the wolf is adaptable. In areas of Europe like Spain, wolves often live on their own, eating small things like rabbits, mice, even fruit and mushrooms. There may be several wolves in an area, sometimes brothers and sisters, and they meet up from time to time in their travels. They greet each other and then go their separate ways.

Scientists who have studied them in the wild report that wolves in a pack are friendly towards each other. When two members of the same pack meet, they greet each other excitedly. Their tails go up, they rub each other, they push their noses into each other's fur. They chase each other, they wag their tails, they make excited high-pitched squeaking noises. One puts its chin on another's back. In short they appear to recognize each other as individuals that are pleased to see each other.

Signals of strength

The pack works as a unit, but the individuals often challenge each other to establish who is 'top dog'. A stronger wolf will make a stiff-legged approach. It will stand its full height and raise its tail. A weaker wolf will crouch close to the ground when approached by a stronger wolf. It may put its tail between its legs or it may even roll belly up as a sign of its submission. If the two fight, they do so by chasing and slamming their bodies into one another. Both wolves bare their teeth: one in aggression, the other in a 'grin' which means 'I am friendly, don't attack me'. Finally the stronger wolf will stand over the weaker and growl a serious growl. Vicious fighting is uncommon. It happens most often when the pack encounters a wolf they do not know.

Wolf territory

To establish a **territory** wolves mark objects in it with their scent. They urinate on bushes, tree trunks, stones and stands of grass. By doing this they establish a piece of ground as belonging to their pack. Scent-markings carry masses of information. They can tell a wolf which other wolves have been there recently; whether they were of the same pack or not; and even whether they were hungry or well fed. If the scent is that of another pack then the wolf will almost certainly 'over-mark' the spot to warn the strangers to keep out. This is how the borders or **boundaries** of the territory are set up.

A pack's territory will vary during the year. On the open **tundra** of North America the wolves' prey of caribou migrates hundreds of

Rocks are natural boundary points and are often used by wolves for scent marking.

A Mexican wolf smells the scent of another pack member.

kilometres and the pack will sometimes move with them. Where prey is scattered, large territories of up to 320 km² may be needed. Its borders are not really marked and will change with the seasons. It is only when there are young cubs that the territory has a centre. At this time of year, the adults may go out to the far reaches of their ground in search of food, but they will always return to the den site. In forests and on islands wolves have much more defined territories, and they will defend them to the death. On Isle Royale in Lake Superior, US, a pack was once seen killing an outsider wolf that had strayed into their patch.

Wolf howl

Wolves make many different sounds including growls, whines, whoofs and barks. But the howl is their characteristic cry. If one wolf howls then all howl, often harmonizing with slightly different notes. People do not agree as to why wolves howl. It may be to assemble the pack and to get everyone in the mood for hunting. It may be to locate each other, for example when brother and sister get separated in the forest. Almost certainly it warns other packs to keep away from their territory. A howl can carry up to 8 km–10 km. As no two wolves will howl the same note at the same time, the variety of sound makes the pack seem bigger and more formidable!

How wolves hunt

Wolves are usually hungry. Most animals are, except those that are very large, such as lions, and which can gorge themselves, and even they become famished again in a day or two. There is a Russian saying, 'A wolf is fed by its feet', and it is true a wolf is often on the move in search of food. They are great travellers, perhaps covering 48 km a day to track down prey during the cold months.

The North American moose can be larger than horses, but wolf packs may hunt them successfully.

Left *Wolves are flesh eaters and will consume almost any kind of bird or mammal.*

Prey is often found by its scent. Downwind, a wolf can smell a deer or a wild boar several kilometres away, and then the pack gradually works its way towards it. The pack will split up, with some animals becoming flankers, going round the sides so that the prey cannot escape so easily. Sometimes the wolves will crouch and stalk slowly. Their camouflage is good, even out in the open, but in the end they will have to make the final rush. If their prey runs, then there are many powerful runners ready to keep up with it. If it turns and fights with its slashing tusks or antlers, then the

wolves will use every scrap of their agility to keep out of the way and so avoid getting hurt. But in many cases, especially with large animals like moose, the wolves will give up rather than tackle a strong, healthy, and potentially dangerous, individual: better to go hungry and live to hunt another day.

The pack is most suited to hunting big animals like white-tailed deer, Dall sheep, caribou, red deer, moose and musk ox. To see wolves hunting among a herd of musk ox is one of the most remarkable sights. Musk ox are massive and tower above the wolves, forming a defensive circle of formidable and heavy horns. If a wolf is caught by one of the horns it will be tossed, trampled and killed. The extraordinary thing is that the wolves can sometimes get to the calves by panicking the herd and cutting them out.

Wolves eat on average 3 kg–4 kg of meat a day. They waste little of a **carcass**, crushing the bones to get the marrow, eating fragments of bone along with hair and skin. They feed fast, seldom remaining long near the kill. They hurry back to their cubs to give them their share. Later they will lie up in cover for a while to digest their meal, before starting off again in search of the next one.

Wolves do not only hunt large animals, however. In many places in Europe, for example, humans have hunted out the red deer, the roe deer, chamois and wild boar, and the wolf has to make do with smaller fare. So they go for mice and voles, sniffing about in the grass and then pouncing on them with their paws. They will eat fruit too, including figs, blackberries and grapes. Grass can be part of their diet, too; they may use it to scour their digestive tract in the same way that a cat may eat grass if it feels unwell. Where food is scarce the pack members may disband to hunt individually, but it will generally re-form when things improve.

A European wolf in pursuit of a brown hare. Generally, wolves prefer larger prey.

Wolf cubs

The wolves' mating season is in the spring. By this time they have established their places in the pack, and it is generally the top male and top female that will become the parents of the new cubs.

By June, after a pregnancy that lasts about 63 days, the she-wolf is ready to give birth. She searches out a place in which to have her cubs. She may excavate a den, or she may find a cave in the rocks, or she may make use of an old porcupine den or badger's set. But just as often, she chooses a patch of heather, or a dry ditch, or simply a stand of long grass in which to settle down to give birth to an average litter of five or six cubs.

Wherever the cubs are born, they must be well hidden, for they are blind and deaf and can only just crawl far enough to find milk from their mother's teats. Dark in colour, they look just like domestic puppies. They weigh approximately 0.5 kg and drink about 300 mL of milk a day. The she-wolf is often exhausted after giving birth and for hours at a time the family simply sleeps.

Between two and three weeks after birth, the cubs' eyes open, they begin to hear, and they become more mobile. If they are out in the open, it can be a hazardous time. Golden eagles, bears and even foxes will snatch one if they can. But even in the protection of a den, a wolf's life is seldom without danger from humans. In European countries, such as Greece and Spain, if a shepherd sees a she-wolf out on the hill, and notices that she's suckling cubs from the size of her teats, he will try to follow her back to her den. Once the rough location of a den is known, the shepherd will bring dogs to find the cubs. Cubs may be killed there and then, or they may be taken through the village, and the villagers asked for money. This is an old custom that is inexcusable today. The wolf is a protected species in Europe, and the damage it does to domestic stock is limited.

When they are one-month old, the cubs leave the denning area. The she-wolf will hide them in the grass or bushes while she goes out

A day-old wolf cub sucks milk from its mother. It is blind and deaf for the first weeks of life.

to hunt. The cubs become a focus for the whole pack now, as they demand more and more food. All the adults show a strong interest in the cubs. When they arrive back from hunting they regurgitate food from their stomachs. The cubs jump up and lick their muzzles and faces, begging for food. This tells the adults that the cubs are submissive but hungry. This is the time that the cubs become part of the wolf pack. Before they are 12 weeks old, they will have established who is top cub; but more importantly they will have established strong emotional bonds with each other and with the adults. For 10 months or so, the adults will feed the youngsters before they

After the birth of her cubs, a she-wolf takes a day or two to recover her strength.

satisfy their own hunger. After that they will all hunt as a pack together for almost two years. Later they will split up, with the new adults, particularly the males, going out to form new packs sometimes many kilometres away.

A wolf may live 15 years unless killed by humans first. By that time its teeth will have been worn down to stumps, but the others in the pack may help to keep it alive; its knowledge of the territory and its sense of where prey may be found are often invaluable to them.

The big bad wolf

The wolf has had a bad reputation. The story of Little Red Riding Hood portrays the wolf as a scheming, voracious creature, which gobbles up the grandmother, then dresses up in her clothes in order to try to do the same to Little Red Riding Hood. The werewolf legend has typecast the wolf as a horror movie extra. From stories such as these we get an image of the wolf as an evil hunter of human beings, from whom we have much to fear. But what is the reality behind this?

It is true that, in the past, wolves were a problem, particularly in Europe, where wolves and human populations came into close contact. Before the coming of guns and poisons, wolves were less afraid of humans, and a shepherd could lose a whole flock of sheep in one night. And that could ruin him:

In winter, wolves may come close to villages and towns to scavenge for food.

Wolf children

There are many tales of children being brought up by wolves. The classic one is that of Romulus and Remus, who were two children abandoned in the hills of Italy. They were looked after by a wolf family. Later they grew up to found the city of Rome.

More recently, in the 1920s, two young girls were found with two wolf cubs near a village south west of Calcutta. Three adult wolves were driven off, and the girls aged 18 months and eight years were taken into an orphanage by the Reverend J. A. L. Singh. They could only crawl and would not walk upright. They bit and howled and preferred eating raw meat to cooked food. They hid in darkness if they could. But no-one was able to discover exactly what had happened to them.

The popular children's stories from *The Jungle Books*, written by Rudyard Kipling and published in 1884/5, feature the adventures of Mowgli, a boy who was adopted by wolves in India after they rescued him from a panther. He was later initiated as a full pack member.

he would have no money to pay his taxes and little to feed to his family. So wolves were a real menace and were greatly feared. Now we have the means to keep wolves at bay and it is they who are very wary of us.

What of the charge levelled at wolves, that they attack and kill humans? Occasionally this may have happened. Wolves and stone age people were direct competitors for food. But in historical times it is a rare occurrence. Between 1764 and 1767 wolves in Gevaudan in France attacked almost one hundred people, many of them herdboys. Eventually several wolves were killed, one of which measured a massive 1.7 m from nose to tail. But they were strangely coloured, and the likelihood is that they were the result of wolves

A wolf's ferocious reputation is undeserved, and its teeth are no larger than a similar-sized domestic dog.

cross-breeding with domestic dogs, perhaps guard dogs. At the time, although there were many wolves in France, herdsmen were not normally that worried about them. This was almost certainly an isolated and remarkable incident.

Wolves, like dogs, can catch **rabies** and attack humans. But any animal with rabies behaves recklessly and highly unnaturally, often foaming at the mouth, biting at anything and showing no fear. In North America it has not yet been proved that a healthy wolf has *ever* attacked a human being.

Friend or foe?

When humans first set foot in Europe thousands of years ago, they were hunters much like the wolf. The wolf was an enemy constantly preying on the same food, trying to steal scraps from the camps, perhaps even snatching the odd baby. But over the course of time, and perhaps 12000 years ago, humans discovered a use for the wolf. It may have been that hunters found wolf cubs and brought them back to camp. The less aggressive ones grew up to accept the human group as its pack. Wolves bark at the approach of strangers; the tamed wolves would have done likewise helping to keep the camp safe. Wolves hunt with their pack; and the tamed wolves would have helped humans in their hunts. And so wolves proved useful and humans started to breed those with the charac-

teristics they liked. The key to the wolf's domestication has been that both wolves and humans work in teams: it was quite natural for a wolf to join the team it grew up with.

Wolves were domesticated in North America, China, India and Europe. Different breeding in different places has given us all sorts of different dogs—Eskimo dogs, Pekinese and Chow, greyhounds and sheepdogs. Over the years, breeding has changed the wolf out of all recognition, so that today it is hard to believe that all domestic dogs are directly descended from the wolf. Its wild adult temperament has been bred out of it. Those individuals displaying young wolf cub characteristics have been chosen. By selective breeding it has been made more placid, and it has been bred not to react over-aggressively to unfamiliar situations and people. Curly tails, big eyes and floppy ears have been selected. The wolf bark has been encouraged, while

The Husky dog was bred to work in cold climates. This team pulls a sled in Antarctica.

the howl has been discouraged! There are of course a few exceptions to this: dogs which have been bred for their aggressive behaviour, include the Rottweiller, the Doberman, the Alsatian and other guard dogs.

Some dogs have been changed from wolves so much they cannot behave like them. A spaniel cannot raise its ears in aggression because they are so droopy; so it constantly looks submissive, although it may not be at all. The Old English Sheepdog cannot communicate with expressions on its face because its face is covered with hair. By contrast, the Alsatian looks very little changed from its wolf descendants. But it too has been extensively bred. It is possible to tell this by its much wider chest: a wolf's is much narrower, with the legs closer together than an Alsatian's.

The fundamental characteristic which makes a dog our best friend is its loyalty. It thinks it must stay with its human family to survive just as a young wolf feels it must stay with its pack. That is a common instinct shared by both domestic dog and wolf.

The dingo, now interbreeding with the domestic dog, is no longer pure in many parts of Australia.

Wild dog dingo

The dingo is an ancient breed of domestic dog. It is probably descended from the Indian or the Indonesian wolf. Around 8000 years ago, stone age seafarers took this prehistoric dog with them from Indonesia and landed on the shores of what is now called Australia. When the dingo arrived there were few predators in Australia, only the Tasmanian wolf and the tiger cat and a few other marsupial hunters. With little competition and an endless supply of kangaroos and wallabies to eat, the dingos ran wild. Later thousands of kilometres of fences were put up to keep dingos away from domestic stock.

After many millenia living away from humans, dingos are difficult to tame. They are quite friendly until they are 18 months old, but not easy to cope with after that.

Jackals

Jackals are smaller than wolves. With a shoulder height of around 40 cm–50 cm and a weight of 7 kg–14 kg, they are the size of a large fox. They can be found in south-eastern Europe, across Asia to northern India and over much of Africa.

Jackals are generally thought of as scavengers because they are often seen picking around for scraps either from a kill or on the outskirts of a village. However they are hunters too. They lack the long legs of a wolf and tend to stalk up on their prey. But they can be very agile when it comes to darting after young gazelles. Their technique is to try to scent where the gazelles are lying in the grass and then grab them as they try to escape. Jackals are plucky and determined, and not to be underestimated.

In general, a jackal's diet is more varied than a wolf's. It includes insects like locusts and beetles, plants, carrion, rats, ground-nesting birds and even fruit. In some places they have been found dining on coffee beans and sugar cane. In southern Africa, they may even go down to the sea to feed on young fur seal pups.

Black-backed jackals catch a young springbok.

Opposite *A golden jackal. Smaller than the wolf, jackals are still formidable hunters which travel great distances in search of prey.*

Young jackals are born in dens—sometimes in an old warthog or aardvark hole. They are carefully guarded by one parent while the other goes out to hunt. On their return, the whole family rushes out to be fed, with ears pressed back and tails wagging. The pups press their muzzles against the corners of their parent's mouth, begging for food. The scene is somewhat reminiscent of a wolf family. However, with jackals, there is seldom a pack. They usually live in pairs or even on their own. Jackal pups start to forage for food at eight months and begin to hunt when they are a year old. They may pair the following year and hold a breeding territory of around 10 km², which they will defend against other jackals.

Types of jackal

There are three types of jackal—the black-backed, the golden and the side-striped. Of the three, the golden is probably most like the wolf. They sometimes howl before they hunt and do occasionally occur in packs. They range the furthest—through North and East Africa, India, and southern Russia.

The black-backed jackal has dark back fur which is speckled with grey. It is paler underneath. They live in similar places to the golden jackal. But wherever black-backed and golden jackals occur together, they are careful not to compete with each other. In the Serengeti National Park, Tanzania, the black-backed jackals occupy the wooded thorn tree areas, while the golden jackals hunt on the plains.

The side-striped jackal has a pair of light and dark stripes on each side of its body and a white-tipped tail. It lives in the southern half of Africa.

The prairie wolf

A coyote howls its yelling cry across the Mohave Desert, California.

The prairie wolf or coyote is a species of wild dog which is halfway between a wolf and a jackal. It is called the prairie wolf because it lives in plains, or **prairie**, areas of North America. In the forest regions of the West it is sometimes also called the brush wolf. But at 11 kg–18 kg in weight it is only half the size of a wolf, with smaller feet and ears, and a more slender face. Even though the coyote is more agile than the wolf, wolves will kill them if they find them; for they are competitors and the two seldom co-exist in the same place. Since the wolf has been exterminated from much of North America, there is plenty of space for the coyotes now. They range from Alaska and Canada down to Mexico and Costa Rica. Once absent from the Atlantic coast of northern US, they have spread now to Massachusetts, Michigan and New York State. They live in every type of habitat, from the Rocky Mountains to the Sonoran desert.

The coyote is adaptable and it has moved in close to the **suburbs** of cities rather like the urban foxes of Europe, raiding garbage cans and garbage dumps in order to survive. In one case in New York State a dog owner could not understand why his pet was losing weight, despite the fact that he fed him lavishly. He found out why when he looked out into his garden one evening. Two coyotes had pushed the dog away from his bowl and were wolfing down the contents themselves. They'd been doing this for weeks!

In the wild, the coyote hunts singly or in pairs. They sometimes howl before hunting.

Unlike a wolf, a coyote's howl grows in volume until it becomes what can only be called a yell. Its prey includes mice, jack rabbits and voles. But nuts and fruit including prickly pears can also form part of their diet. Coyotes can pose a threat to domestic stock such as lambs and chickens, but these make up less than one-sixth of their diet.

A coyote pair will bring up their young together in a den (which may be an old badger, skunk or fox burrow) trying to keep them safe from the coyotes' natural enemies

A pair of coyotes survey their territory in the Sonoran Desert, Arizona.

which include the wolf, the golden eagle and the puma. Up to eight young may survive, and they will then strike out in the autumn to establish their own territories. Some may end up on the outskirts of cities. In Toronto there has been a problem with 'coydogs'—crosses between coyotes and domestic dogs. The offspring of such couplings can be aggressive, but the problem now seems to be under control.

African wild dogs

The African wild dog, or hunting dog, is not so closely related to the wolf as are the jackal and the coyote. But to see a pack of hunting dogs fanning out over the plains of East Africa in pursuit of prey leaves one in little doubt about the similarities in their behaviour. Effectively, they are the wolves of Africa!

The African wild dog hunts in a similar way to the wolf. They hunt in packs of up to 25. They approach herds of plains animals like zebra and wildebeeste and test them to see whether there are any weak animals that they might go for. Wolves use exactly the same

A pack of African wild dogs have seized a wildebeeste.

The African wild dog has large litters; in some cases more than one female will have young.

method with musk ox and caribou. When they have identified a meal, then different animals in the pack have different functions. There are lead dogs which spearhead the attack, while the flankers go round the side of the herd to prevent escape.

In a wolf pack everyone knows where they stand—who is stronger and who is weaker. But in an African wild dog pack, there aren't quite the same rules. Wild dogs aren't necessarily dominant or submissive to each other. They don't communicate so much with the expressions on their faces and their body postures as do wolves. In fact the way the pack hangs together is by members regurgitating food for each other! For all these reasons, the African wild dog has not been domesticated like the wolf.

Decline of the hunting dog

In many areas of East Africa, the hunting dog is in decline. This is partly because hunting dogs take domestic stock such as sheep and goats in ranching areas outside the national parks, and partly because hunting dogs have suffered from diseases such as distemper and mange. In areas of the Masai Mara game reserve in Kenya numbers are now down to a handful. In a recent sighting, a pack of just five dogs was observed hunting in a thunderstorm. After a long chase, they downed a Grant's gazelle. Then the two adults sheltered under a tree, leaving their two-thirds grown puppies to feed in the rain. Only when the pups had had their fill did the parents move in to feed off the leftovers.

Wild dogs today

In the past the world's wild dogs have suffered badly at the hand of humans. The story is the same in Europe, Africa and North America. First people hunted all their prey animals, like deer, antelope, buffalo and boar. Then when wild dogs were forced to turn on domestic stock from time to time, people decided to exterminate this unwanted pest. Their fur was sometimes a desirable extra.

It is difficult to estimate how many wild dogs have been killed by humans in the course of history, but it must be millions. It is even more difficult to estimate how many other animals have died as a result of eating poison put down for wild dogs. Ravens, vultures, foxes, kites, eagles, stoats and other carnivores have perished in unknown numbers through ingesting poisons like cyanide and strychnine intended for wild dogs. In North America it is still considered sport to shoot wolves by pursuing them from aircraft, or to chase them on a snowmobile into snow drifts which are too deep for them to run through. The primitive hatred of the wolf dies hard.

Now perhaps the tide is beginning to turn slightly in favour of the wild dogs. As a result of wildlife campaigns, research, and natural history programs we are beginning to realize that predators are not 'bloodthirsty beasts', but individuals each with characters of their own. The message is that every wild dog has a right to live.

Today in Africa, tourists travel hundreds of kilometres for the chance of seeing wild dogs and jackals. In the US it is possible to go out to special areas and hear wolves howling. People come from as far away as Europe to listen to this eerie cry—perhaps because it symbolizes the wilderness that we have lost in our desire to cultivate, or build on, every last piece of the world's surface.

The coyote, ruthlessly poisoned for many years, now has a number of safe sanctuaries.

Inevitably the wilderness will shrink as the human population expands. So the question is whether it is possible for wild dogs to live in settled areas. There are two things we can do. Firstly, we must make sure that there are plenty of *wild* animals for them to hunt. Secondly it is vital that, in wild dog areas, shepherds pen their stock in safely at night, and during the day guard the herd with large domestic dogs. Wild dogs may never become our best friends, but at the very least we need no longer think of them as our worst enemies.

Right *A young wolf plays with cotton grass. Many young wolves struggle to survive their first few years of life.*

Below *In East Africa hunting dogs need all the help they can get if they are to continue to exist.*

Glossary

Boundaries The borders or limits of a territory.

Camouflage Means of disguise often by colour or shading, so that an animal is hidden or hard to see.

Carcass Body of a dead animal.

Carnivore An animal that eats meat.

Cultivate To prepare and use land for growing crops.

Dominant Have command over; be superior to.

Prairie Large treeless area of level or undulating grassland of North America.

Prey Animals that are hunted and killed by other animals.

Rabies Dangerous viral disease often transmitted from one animal to another by biting.

Range Area over which an animal species is scattered.

Regurgitate To bring up digested food from the stomach.

Retract To draw back into the body.

Scavenge To feed on garbage and the remains of dead animals.

Submissive Giving way to more powerful individual.

Suburbs Outlying district of a city.

Territory An area which an animal regards as its own, where it feeds and breeds, and which it defends against others.

Tundra A treeless Arctic region where the soil just below the surface is frozen throughout the year.

Ultrasound Sounds that are higher than the range of human hearing.

Index

The entries in **bold** are illustrations.

Picture Acknowledgements

The publishers would like to thank the Survival Anglia picture library, London, England and the following photographers for the use of photographs on the pages listed:

Jen and Des Bartlett 5, 21, 23; Joel Bennett 20; Jeff Foott 13, 14 (right), 24, 25, 28; John Harris 6; Richard and Julia Kemp 4, 7, 10, 11, 12, 14 (left), 16, 17, 18, 19, 29 (top); Kemp/Finzel 15; R. L. Matthews 26; Matthews/Purdy 29 (below); John Pearson 27; Maurice Tibbles 22; Claude Steelman 8, 9.

About the author

Jeremy Bradshaw studied Zoology at Oxford University in England. He has made more than a hundred natural history and environmental programmes for Survival Anglia, the internationally renowned wildlife film-makers based in Norwich, England, where he is senior producer. He travelled to East Africa to film giraffes, and his previous publications include a book on Animal Giants.